The Little Animal Follow-the-Dots Coloring Book

Roberta Collier

Dover Publications, Inc., New York

The Little Animal Follow-the-Dots Coloring Book is a new
work, first published by Dover Publications, Inc., in 1991.

International Standard Book Number: 0-486-26666-4

Manufactured in the United States of America
Dover Publications, Inc.
31 East 2nd Street
Mineola, N.Y. 11501

Note

This is a book filled with pictures of all kinds of animals. The animals are given to you only partly drawn. It's up to you to fill in the rest of each animal by connecting the dots in each picture. To connect the dots, use a pen or pencil and draw a line from dot 1 to dot 2, from dot 2 to dot 3 and so on until all the dots are connected. You can try to guess what kind of animal is shown in the picture before you connect the dots. There are sayings under each one, including many with a hint to help you guess. Also, there's a list of animals at the back of the book so you can check your answers. When you are finished connecting the dots, you will then have 56 wonderful pictures ready for you to color in any way you want to. You will run into many delightful and some strange animals as you have fun following the dots in the pages of this book—so let's get started!

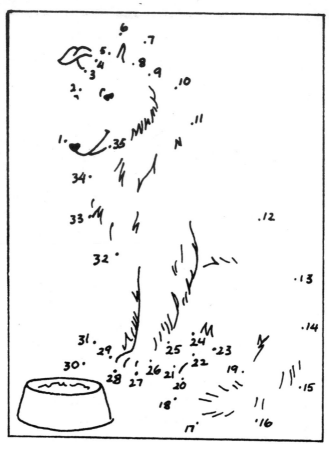

Breakfast is served!

Who's king of the jungle?

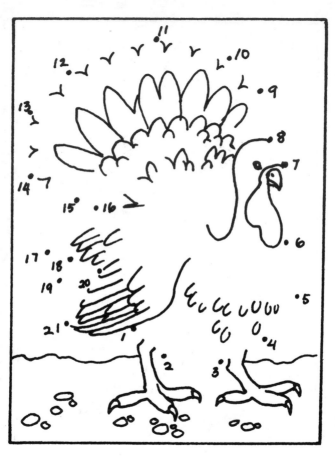

Who's coming over for Thanksgiving?

"Who? Who?"

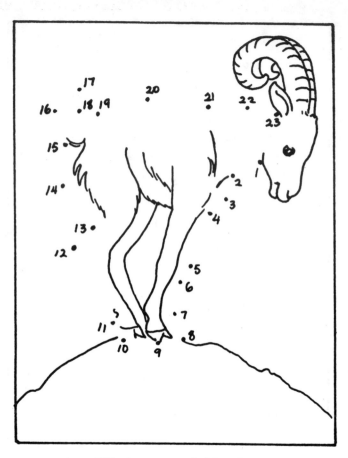

Who's on top of things?

Who's that in the bushes?

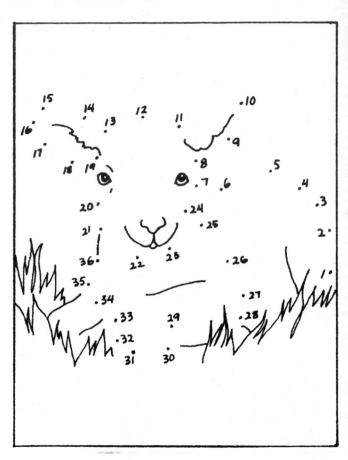

Resting in a field, who might this be?

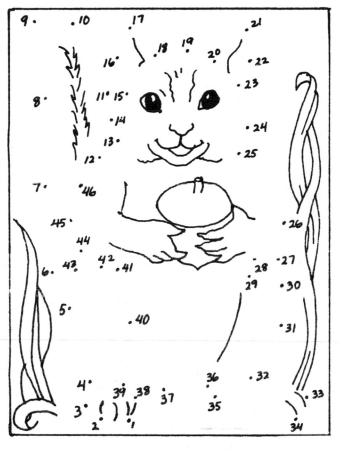

Who's got the acorn?

11

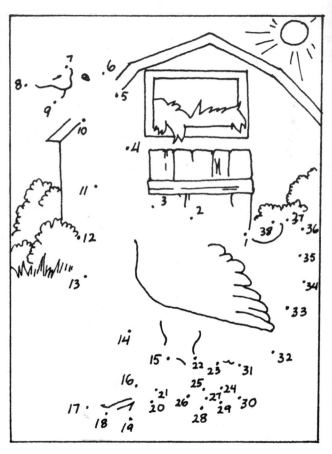

"Honk, honk! Which way to the barn?"

Where's Mom?

"Cheep! Cheep!"

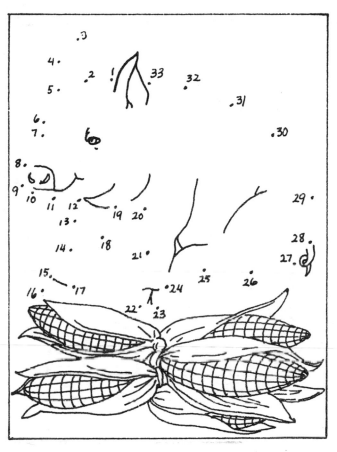

Dinner's ready! And who is here to eat it?

15

Who's found an egg?

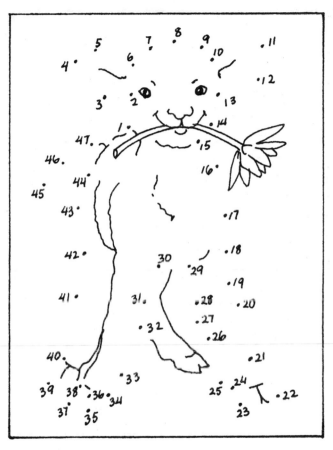

Who's been eating the daisies?

Who just came out of the egg?

Who's the masked one?

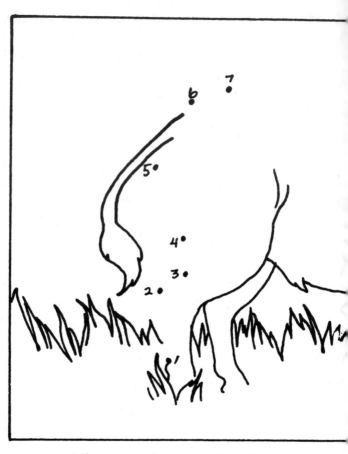

Who roams the grassy plains?
[Pages 20 and 21 contain a single picture.]

Who's in the flowerpot?

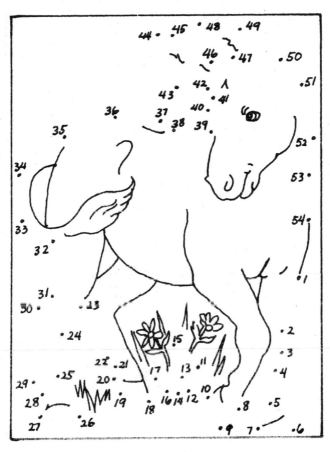

Who's the sure-footed one?

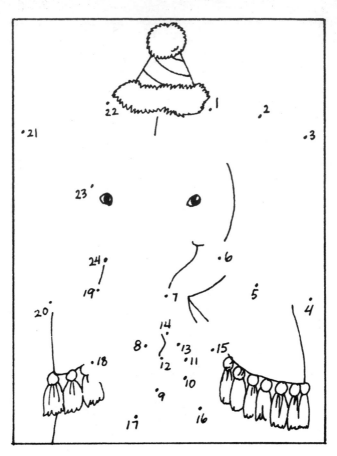

Look at the youngest circus clown!

Someone small is living on the forest floor.

What little creature has been eating the corn?

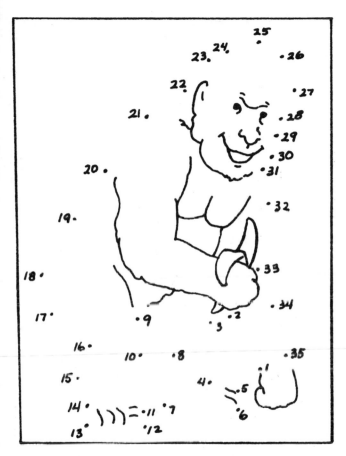

Who has found a favorite food?

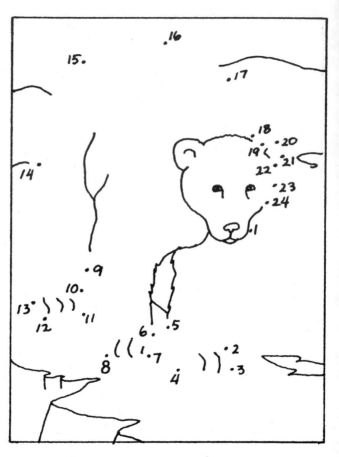

Who roams about the frozen North?

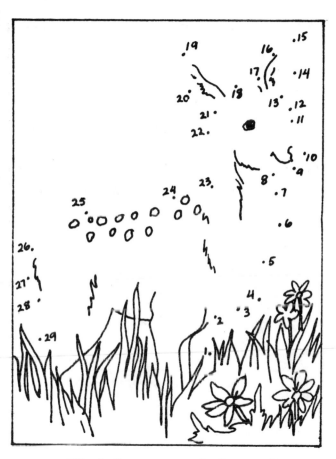

Who's the youngster in the grass?

Who has a pretty shell?

This happy fellow lives in Borneo.

Who is man's best friend?

Two playful creatures—what are they?

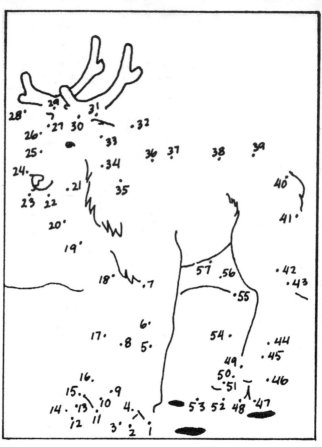

Crossing lands of snow and ice—who is this?

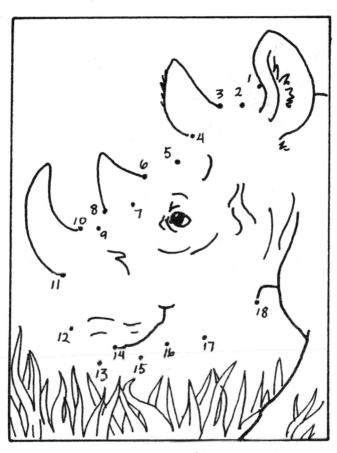

Who has big horns and lives in Africa?

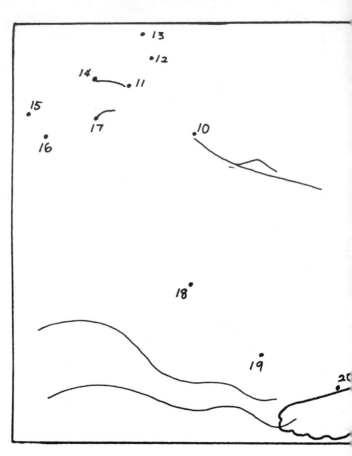

Who lives in the ocean deep?
[Pages 36 and 37 contain a single picture.]

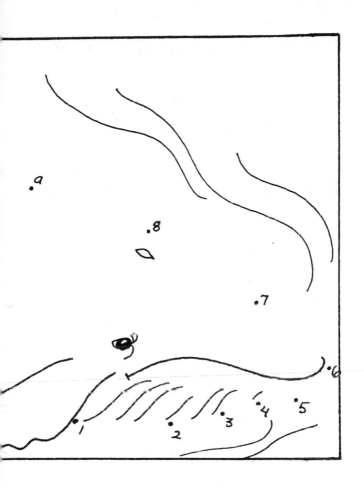

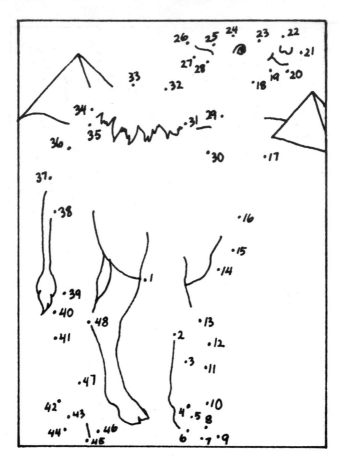

Who goes for days without water in the desert?

Who's that with the mother pony?

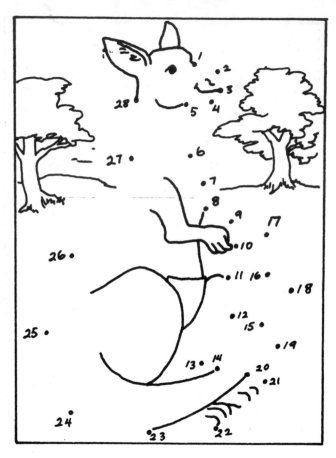

Someone has a hopping good time in Australia.

Who's that up in the eucalyptus tree?

Someone's nibbling on a little seed.

Someone is hiding among the buttercups.

Who's got a coat of spiny quills?

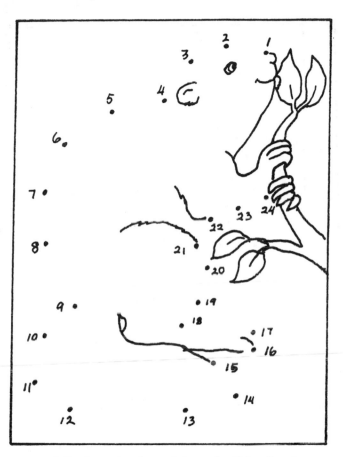

Who's gathering sticks to build a dam?

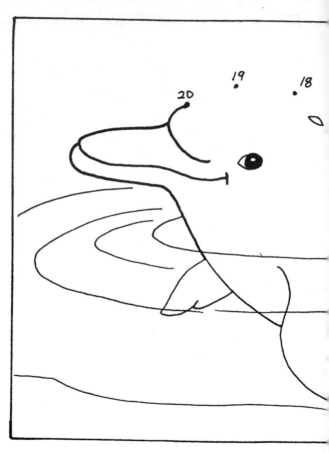

Who's the playful one in the water?
[Pages 46 and 47 contain a single picture.]

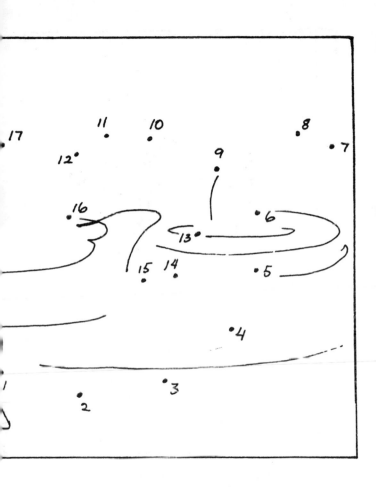

47

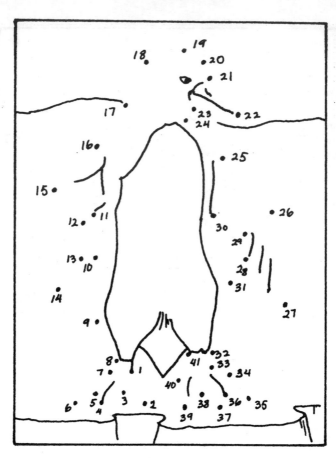

Who likes to dive into icy water?

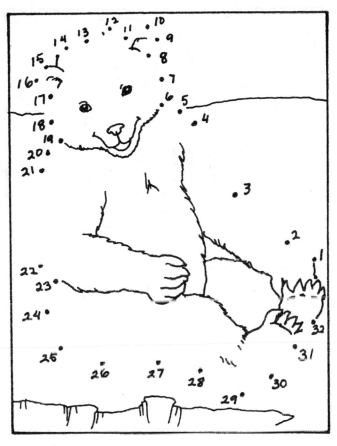

Somebody else likes cold and ice. Guess who.

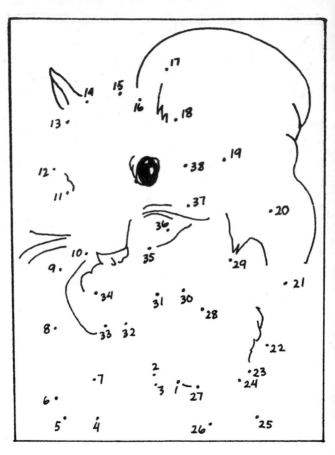

Someone likes to eat nuts.

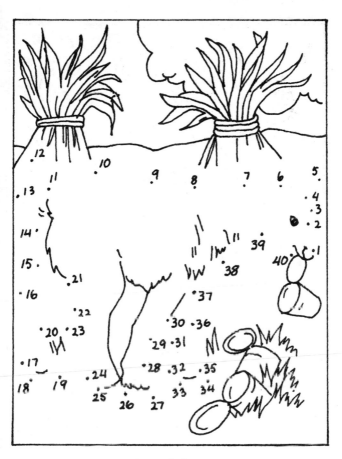

Lunchtime!

Who's the big croaker?

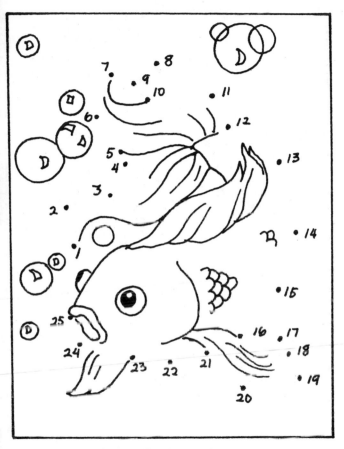

Who's blowing bubbles?

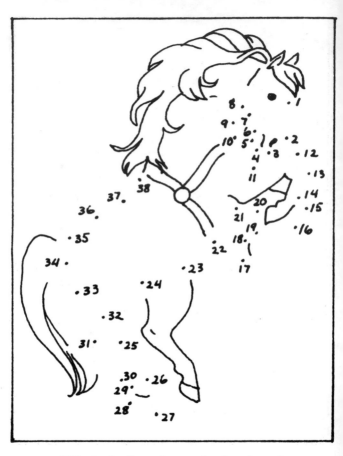

Who's the best dancer in the circus?

Who gives milk to the farmer?

Who's swinging high up in the vines?

Who's the little stinker?

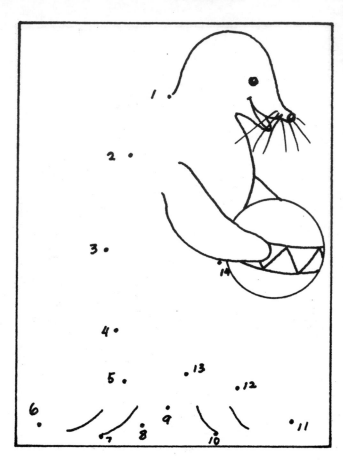

Who has a ball at the circus?

Who's that perched on a limb?

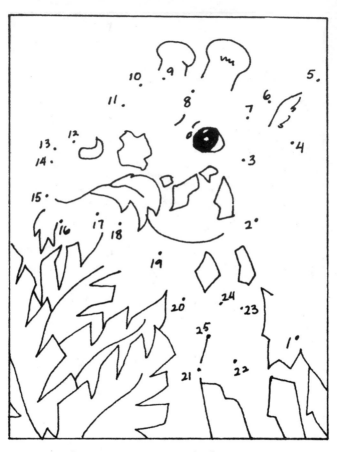

Someone can get to the leaves at
the tops of trees.

Who loves feasting on bamboo shoots?

Who's found a house in a hollow tree?

Identifying the Pictures

When you follow the dots, these are the animals you will find.